The Stone and the Square

THE STONE AND THE SQUARE

DUSTIN PICKERING

Hawakal
PUBLISHERS
New Delhi | Calcutta

HAWAKAL PUBLISHERS
70 B/9 Amritpuri, East of Kailash, New Delhi 65
33/1/2 K B Sarani, Mall Road, Calcutta 80

Email info@hawakal.com
Website www.hawakal.com

Cover art by Shutterstock

Cover designed by Bitan Chakraborty

First edition(paperback) March 2021

ISBN: 978-81-950350-3-8

Price: INR 300 | USD 12.99

for
Timberlake Àngel and Henry

God writes straight with crooked lines.

Portuguese proverb

ACKNOWLEDGMENTS

"fingertips" was first published by *Setu,* Western Voices edition 2021. Many thanks to Scott Thomas Outlar for selecting this poem.

"a beautiful scream" and "i want the world to be infinite for you" from *Witch Hazel* were published in *The Punch Magazine,* World Poetry and Prose Portfolio, October 2020. Many thanks to Sudeep Sen for selecting these poems.

The first section was initially a chapbook entitled *Baby, It's Cold Outside.*

CONTENTS

IT'S COLD OUTSIDE

in silence 15
night craving 16
bluebirds 17
harm's shadow 18
child's eyes 19
anger of the dark 20
parcels of many 21
beyond reason 22
timelessness is not brocade 23
i will not forget 24
sophistry and artifice 25
undoing 26
pain & pleasure 27
timid fascination 28
the hideous 29
addressing this science 30
minarets 31

THE STONE AND THE SQUARE

building a home 35
shadowed 36
never think 37
secrets 38
homes 39
fingertips 40
dreamsong of tears 41
door of memory 42
the feast 43
forgotten poppies 44
forgotten peonies 45
orchids 46

WITCH HAZEL 49-80

Hello!

The first section (*It's Cold Outside*) was composed during the Great Freeze of Texas 2021. My electricity was shut off for three days intermittently. I charged my phone during the breaks. I used its light to write poems under my blanket, where my breath kept me warm as temperatures plummeted.

Section Two (*The Stone and the Square*) is composed of various poems on love to create unity with the rest of the book. *Witch Hazel* is a book in itself, also on the theme of love.

Many thanks to *Hawakal Publishers* for their dedication to poetry and art. Thanks to Kiriti Sengupta for being a mentor in this project.

Dustin Pickering
24 February 2021
Houston, Texas

it's cold outside

in silence

In one drop of water are found all the secrets of all the oceans;
in one aspect of You are found all the aspects of existence.
—Kahlil Gibran

within my chest
i lock the tenderest treasure.
together we oscillate
— our highs and lows —
gathering momentum as we live.

behind the golden saturnine door
is a treasure
neither of us can unmake or abandon:
in our hearts, love is deepened
like gravity
on a moral arc.

water or rain,
i will love you with fervor:
forever, the secret will be kept
in silence.

night craving

your night is my night
we are soft as winter snow,
warm as joy in pride.

lovemaking is fire in the wind—
storms of fear and fragility
fall from my skin.
into your eyes i lay weeping.

the dusty horizon of our spirit
rises from its morning threshold:
one longing in eternal floods.

and though the night craves our silence,
we do not give it.

bluebirds

and though ive waited for these crimson years…
bluebirds are flying from your eyes
into the trapeze of fear.

a human world is built on longing;
satisfaction is a sphere divine
like an eyeorb, stoical yet serene,
clutching what it perceives.

i write a sonnet to your breath—
while you sleep, i float awkwardly
   to your lips.
psyche of suffering, torn by lot,
my candle is ashen by the hour's end.

harm's shadow

how can i listen without love?
do i know the tongues that declare,
declare worlds absent of life?

i fill the void with tears of sleep.
thoughts do not comfort me in the deep.
lost in lands of forgetting,
my heart angelical sorrow keeps.

i am brought to the brine of grief,
close to the silence of an egg.
when swarms of raging demons fly,
i kiss the tornado of your eyes.

the only magic is this star's listlessness.
paradoxes of sweet earth remain—
yet touch the silent wind, no,
because i am ill to harm's shadow.

child's eyes

strangers in the dusk
an afternoon promise
                                        freedom of light
without arms we gaze into darkness

oracular bustles of young words
fill the child with virgin sight:
          what he sees offers slender temerity.

if only a shy gaze could see
the longer offerings of time!
but we fill the heart of humankind
with spectacular rhyme.

anger of the dark

shadows empty of flight
from objects of mirth:
sun and mistletoe
are not for regal birth.

limp longings lurch past graveyards—
wreck the willful ship of skeletal host.

hope is not at war yet—
it is still tumescent in its voice,
filled with anger of the dark.

parcels of many

a light in the night
to succumb to the drum
of insolent merriment—

frozen in time while pastures of plenty
devolve into parcels of many
broken and divided by crucibles of time.

discordant emptiness.
the night declares winterland.

beyond reason

what is day when twilight
is so deep?
night sweeps the plenary array
from a sky perfect and thoughtful.
presented by god in finest decadence,
though nature is never overwhelming.

like a sea of renewal
the cold flitters through—
treading our comfort, denying its fruit.

the pastures of plenty suffer the harvest,
for a time.
there is nothing beyond reason but a rhyme.

timelessness is not brocade

the mind engages what it will—
talk like a viper and feel the spit.
rushes of fear and forgetting
fap against the stolen artifice of time.

the haunting is connotation-wise.
there are no dreams to resurface
from this celebrity brine.

an ego is undoing its blouse,
sequestering the foreigners of years.
it is naked and content,
ready for contest and sacrament.

we batter our eyelashes with foolishness.
timelessness is not brocade of birth.

i will not forget

shelter me; it is a derelict posture
to imitate.

your eyes, love; they are lamps
of mercy.

shelter me, love; kiss my oblivion
clean as a whisper.

i will not forget our weeping.

sophistry and artifice

the tulips were burned by poison
while your clever lips spoke widely.

i penned my fears and fortunes
but only the devil could hear.

challenge me again, truth:
i will not succumb to your folly.

thoughts profoundly disturb me in loneliness.
i will not be dismayed by ancient posturing.

take your Aristotle and Plato:
the sea will melt their tears.

undoing

I have written many lies
so anticipate my disguise.
havoc is a phantom paradise.

eclipse the darkness of fear
and hold tightly your own rage.
the only trust is your silence.

do not weasel through the window,
my satin friend.
you signal to the many
to undo amends.

pain & pleasure

pain recoils from itself,
chasing beauty in the garden of woe.
behind the safety of your eyes
lies my dormant whisper.

o brain, and beacon of love:
carry promises to the river.

*

pleasure multiplies in darkness—
seeking stones or silences.

*

eyes only hold the truth
in disbelief:
a willful suspension.

timid fascination

when the shattering police of Necessity
claim my life,
i am left bereft of midnight.

keeping watch over my workings
is timid fascination
for peril is risky to my dream.

my city works angelically to temper
the excesses of fear
in my heart,

but i am a small man with only one child.

And that child is my being-in-the-world.

the hideous

blackened by tolerance and rage—
against this storm of incomprehensibility.

do i suffer a pronoun or two
to shed my light?

steal this steel engine of trembling:
your eyes are my gladiators.

wakefulness does not charm the hideous.

addressing this science

hills of sanctimonious fear
flagellate my brow,
incomprehensibility.

snow thickens the night
with waiting—
and i can satisfy my heart.

while the bandits pass the light
from subliminal to subliminal,
i am without sweetness.

matter-of-factly I am facing dread.

minarets

a hour with no power
and the night is still phantom-like,
kissing brides of freedom.

is freedom risk or do we know
what linkage is taken?

how does the coin illuminate being
to suffuse the wound?
clocks wounded and tried with passion,
they lay down their hands in minutes.

minarets oblivious to power's demagoguery,
shut to the slight,
we only know what they recommend.

the stone and the square

building a home

together we build this bulging sight,
home of our arching bodies—
where together we fill with delight
sensual dimension of our predilections.

your mind is my stone;
my body is your square.
together we form isolated currents
in the thinly wrought air.

shadowed

your eyes, shadowed with longing—
this angel of distance, sign of thought
in love.

your mind encases me to protect our heart—
together we are one and never apart.

your eager eyes, eyes sensing horizons,
venerate with motion
all that holds the sky in.

i cannot hold this thought more clearly,
that you are the one who wishes for my silence
on the escape hatch of light.

do you understand now?
how am i the one you trust
over all others?

never think

sounds emerge from your lips,
a silence i never think to kiss,
an otherness of longing…

i cast temples their stones while you
knit pastimes from our togetherness.
our union is permanence seeking permanence.

we build castles in the sky
while the world tells lies to the sighs
of our tongues to dismiss what beauty
clearly is held in the night.

secrets

will you expose your deepest secret to me
as a wound unwinding its bandage?
does blood despise the one for whom it
bleeds?

oh, but my mind is haunted with your
thoughts—
we are one silent fire burning at the fore,
a torch of Tantalus.

the night casts a deep purple fascination
across our kissing lips.

homes

hearts decorate the hearth
my life is darkness and warmth
in this little hellflame
of my meager existence

i crash cold against the waters.

*

silence is my motion
i keep the fabric of time
clean with my tears

*

we know time by how it moves
we know space by how it communicates.

fingertips

fingertips touch the flame,
blue and gold,
like yesterday's pleasure
in the spiritual house.

when we return we are only
victims of loose learning.

the loam carries us from saint
'to sage to sorry,
and we dwell on dreams
of coal and ice.

the night air breathes into us
the life we have chosen.

dreamsong of tears

the sun shines
a glorious Otherness—
tepid warmth

nuts and flowers
hang in oblivion
like a dreamsong of tears

as we perch our souls
together on the bough
cherries fall from our bosoms

and the light absorbs
what little doubt we had
concerning each other

door of memory

a bed where we promise
forgetfulness

moonlight strikes like a bow
balancing the night
on a hinge of memory

trees grateful for the light
reach for the edge of night
losing all trust in themselves

searching for the perfect music
has consequences

the feast

Our bodies consume the flame:
an animal of fear and faith,
a furnace of Creation
the grandeur of which contemplates.

Her eyes, like startled doves,
cast uncertaintics and hurt—
we stand alone together, naked,
her breasts poised and alert.

The knowledge we seek together:
incontrovertible yet aggrieved
as hunter to his hunted—
the Lord mends with sympathy.

Her voice burns effulgently
kissing the silence of surcease,
illustrious sun illuminating presence—
togetherness of this feast.

forgotten poppies

I once ached but aching was futile.
My pains were simple reminders of emptiness.
I adopted my own fears ad memories
to anticipate a language of the Lord.
He stood above me, aching and alone,
and we knew each other as the light
knew darkness, reaching eternally within.

These eyes shone ostensibly for my Part
in such a phantom salvation:
His love embodied my body,
thickening intensities of strife.
Immortal wounds I suffered beautifully
to enrapture a field of forgotten poppies.

forgotten peonies

Something greater than smallness
exists for the pleasures of anticipation.
Her sighs and griefs remind me
to treat the worshippers gingerly.
Pity that the world shears its best
and highest coats and crosses.

*

Love is the highest grant of loneliness
in the land.

orchids

the sunbeam broke its leg
crossing the threshold
of your invention:

to reach the bold symbol
of your love,
the sunbeam leapt from the glass

of the window
into the vase of my gaze.

witch hazel

what a beautiful scream
of lust, circumference breaking.
it doesn't announce itself.

and she walks wounded,
skirting the trees of humility.
fallen torch, a thought

in sanctimonious shroud.

the world loves her charms
and sweet sophistication,

but in humility—

she is only doing God's work.

I want to tell you
I love you
but my frenzied heart
cannot escape its fearful solitude.
Your love is my heart turned gay
and sweet as a peach.
The measure of your dreams,
deep longing and bliss,
love's countenance
sets her bashful eyes to rest.

When I read you my poem
you will see the stars.

I want the world to be infinite
for you
so that your heart will live for love:
within your spiritual complexion
rest roses of beatitude.

A fire of fury never lounges to escape—
only you tend to the garden
before you, an angel lush with crimson.
I seek your love like a phantom
of splendor—

growth comes with our sheltering.

My heart remains broken
A healer's art resides in your breast
Sweet eyes of salvation
          lay their gestures to my mind—
phantom archangels sing swift silences.

Green rivers of fertility
                              flow
                    from your presence—
you weep for my own forgetting.

However I have not seized your love
from spaces in the dream.
All longing is united
                              beyond
          a common theme.

You open the window
for wind to follow through
like vast trumpets of abandonment
declaring empty
war.
We've been here before—
yet the light warms our future
as it passes warmed by the Lord.

We can hide in terrors unknown—
or we can drink vintage wine
until the morrow.

The shell, haunted, is our prison cell.
They know our bodies
but not the light.

Old rose of magical mystery,
does she captivate me?
The silence of her loom
shields me from error.
Wisdom knows nothing of wages—
give gladly,
                    never return.

I return in silence
hoping to presume your faith
in eyes of my times
an era of wishing away mistakes.

when the stillness reckons
with night's cold epiphanies,
stars will sling blindness in truth.

Together we are a union of bird and fish—
subtle sloth vanishes.
We hunger for the emptiness of touch.

An anthem is absorbed
in my heart.
It is you, love, unwilling to part.
A song of the flesh
        lingers lustfully like a river.
Quiets the sound of angry venom
        sequestered by our opiate minds.

If you sleep and relax
it is me holding your hand.
Night fills us with furtive blessings—
pages from our book fall and burn
like time's empty wounds.

We don't know each other
across deserts or mountain peaks—
our rain between hours mystifies our pain.

A rose is a heart unfolding
fill'd with secrecy in bloom—
when most of midnight placates
the inner worm of fear

    our union avows no floods,
    no entropy,
    no dense light unseen.

Delightful music engages our phantom elements.
Poverty is not the doubt I crave.
My thoughts are enslaved
by every wound you gave.

Worried hush cannot silence our trust.
What neither of us say,
the stars bid us to unfold.

Your lips fancy words I cannot say.
Under your rich canopy
I will envision Nature's fool—
myself by proxy stemmed

and sheltered in the earth.

You string my heart together
like vines,
from this wasted dreaming
we birth a dance of youth.

You are my companion—
eager for rain

we cry silently
on the plain.

I'm waiting for you to comfort me.
Bliss, come, my darling isn't here.
Her eyes know the seat of my knowledge.
Passion's cape hides the reality.

I raise my heart to the sky—
unfathomable riches burn in your lips
          and eyes
where my image is transposed.

The shutters of my imagination
still the starlight of your dreams—
I have stolen the tears
again, love:

                    while we slumber
                    in solitude's wake.

I waltz the winter rooms
through brocade of empty silence
testing the veracity of death.

"only to sense your love
fading into tears"

as death is my continuous companion
when language fails,
crossing the waters to paradise
is my last resort

until your eyes cease the watering.

unhindered, these words:
unchaste my poison
                                        picked from prairies

diluted by dust, shameless.

a heart's grandeur
                                        is baleful joy

maladies of strength and weakening.

power's silence
                              shakes the blossoms
                              from your eyes.

Take my ransom for granted
while I kiss the stone—
feeling along is not alone.

Beauty invokes grief
through the prism of conscience.
When light streaks cleverly
to show the motes for scrambling cowards,

            my heart is struck, o!
            your eyes are amazed horizons.

Such a glimpse of priceless prayer
awakens the growing cosmic urge.
I expand my love year by year;

you are always more than meaningful.

The door was slammed in my face.
I turned and you are there,
holding fire and flakes of forgetting.

I forgive my captor—
her heart is slim and dreary.
Warm my salty tears;
I want to bed free of shadows.

The only thing more precious than love
is the experience of love.

Gravity pulls us together
by holding us apart.
Thru winter worrisomeness
we wait as we embark—

the ship is cast to light…
empty thoughts prevail
over dream's perfection.

Such is not what it seems.

All grief—
unstated, what is an expectation
gathering its flowers?

How do we know what is secret to the world.

What's a fevered touch to the soul,
brimmed with glee.
Are we still alive?

Is this a dungeon lacking all its torture?

I cannot see future tense:
for love is my lobotomy…
I trust your trysting swords
but I will stand on fallow ground.

Cannibalize this thirsty heart.

Fire no more—
your eyes teach the passing fears
within me.

I do not see the doldrums striking
at the master's door.
What is this terror? Lucid dreaming?

Life is a mystery and you are its hope.

How can I complain about doves
and eagles
                                        when your stars
                              blind me completely?

I am in darkness while waiting for your soul
to reach across the rivers of form.

The moon turns yellow and thinks
the graces of time
belong to this earth—
yet moons cannot think
unless possessed with love.

Turn my empty face from the truth.
Again, loneliness is not a vice.

Her tenderness—sweetly perfumed con-
science,
I study the ways of love.

The thought of eternity opening a door
to enlighten shame
never occurred to me as well as now.

List your thorough dream:
    an ocean foaming with hope
    texture of light to see the priests
    sunshine leaving its impressions

Love, love and salt:
nothing is as bitter as loss
and nothing is deeper than fear.

I sing the lullaby that tames
your inner tiger,
friendly beast of passion—
his glad heart is Spirited Circumference.

Come, live, and see the fear swallowed
like Jonah,
and ready for redemption.
His shame in not-doing what must be done—
reluctance and fear, closed chaos.

Wings will take us in like a home.

I sing the cold wind
and we sleep in the silence
of your heart.
I hear the dreaming you present
and know we are always and forever
something beyond ourselves.

Burn the witch hazel, its compounded memory
of lost life.

Grief isn't a shadow.

Memory is uncanny—
I cannot forget our losses,
they are ours always.

Stretched taut as a canvas
your soul is sunshine to the bright eyes
of wisdom.

Turn, turn again. We rest.

Reality trimmed to opinion,
not of solace:
nothing shames.

a tree that stands in winter—
bunked for a year.
the hidden light of winter
resurrects the empty shining.

bliss covers so much mountain
as we stand in rivers of silence:

her hair is colored graphite
split to the name.

If we grow from the night—
see only the sunflowers and their bashfulness—
nothing of rhythm will untie human bounty.
we already know the fleeing thoughts.

infinite lies curse this vanity
of human sorrow—
the land is wet with honey and rain,
scent of blossoms arouse suspicion.

one more time do we speak
before I leave for the war.

wishing me well, battle-hardened
as I return to my senses:
you will quietly praise God.
I walk into the fires for your clandestine purpose.

Secrets are never unspoken.
They treat touches as flight.

music engages in the flux of law—
anticipating night.
Do we belong to this earth?
Whatever was ours?

I would like to make an unusual request—
stay by me, never turning, never:
keep watch over my disappointment and dream.

let me be the divining rod tonight—
foolishness can escape from clatter mouths
but I tempt the water from the ground.

ah, but here you are found in sleep—
thoughtless, content.

images appear of fear and forgetting.
things the morning will not tell.
the sun passes through the curtain
to embrace your loving face.

Apollo, will you wait for me?
how do I find you when you are silent,
o Love, my Beloved?

maidenhead refutes, silent carcass of the dawn
wakes again from foamy assurance—
a craving for your love satisfies through the years.

the sea turns and turns—
Neptune dances in command of the waters.

I allow myself certain despair
so that I may appreciate the dawning light.
breathless ardor—
sink to the deep hedonism of our world—
all others are lost to its trenches.

we seek pleasure because pain is not enough—
as we sift the stolen ashes of her open adolescence,
clouds take flight through the monstrous crags.

who is escaping our torchlit eyes?
we bend together to seek mandates of Mass.

I'll keep traveling the wounds you built for yourself—
a flat earth, mercy: too many worries
to doll up this empire of waste.

dry, dry, speak water:
scale the frontiers of nothingness.

She hints her salubrious mask
to a direction I cannot seek.
Touched by permanence,
our story will not cease.

Have you more to cry over than me?
Has loss hurt you in a passing gaze?
There are no prisoners walking free—
our warden commands the sea.

Voluminous mistakes are clumsily made
until this river, chaste, dreamy—
swallows its own currents in a pith of pride.

Like seeds to the wind we float high
reaching the central assent of life.
We fear nothing as we embark together
against enemy foundations.

The world we know is a hoax
conflating time and pronoun.

When the essentials return to our laughter—
when, only when—
we will fir our love in a bright box
that holds our soul hidden in rapture.

You are deep and tired;
I, languid and wise.

If rivers flow toward the earth's end,
then the two of us must last forever.

The burning never ceasing—
grief, such slant knowledge;
truth, such a mean imbecile.

Are we born to merely suffer!
Are we masters of the pride we cherish?
How do we know if we are forever?

Heaven belongs to you:
it's perplexed radiance
of jewels and gold.
You are an act of remembrance.
I knew you were staving off the seeds.

Keep away from the hearth,
o burning child:
your impulse is forgiven.
God is in the sagacious pen
composing these verses.

Why do we ask for more?

Whither on the wall is damnation—
I don't conceive heaven, it is lost to my eyes.

Where shall I go? I leave the night before
to you and your hopes.

If I am truly lost, I cannot be found
by your wandering thoughts.

Hell is empty and dark, full of blood.

I am your parable and penumbra.
Words are put into your mouth
by my holy desires.

We are free only if we are together.

I do not entrap my spider
because her dreams are lies.
I entrap her because I am stronger.

Her quiet poise does not scare me.

Your eyes center me to the starry night.
When I am lost to failure—
remind me what success is ahead.
I wage a silent war at the crucifixion.
Christ understands my pain—

only he knows this depth of loneliness
as I am entangled in the web,
infinite and merry,
kissed by the wayfarer again.

Epithalamium

The fly, a lustre,
bright diamond on the sea.

sing the hymen
sing, sing the hymen

the world is cold
birds hang on empty air
like dreams forgotten

and each death is rebirth
the fly, a lustre,
count me as lost.

www.ingramcontent.com/pod-product-compliance
Lightning Source LLC
La Vergne TN
LVHW091619170726
843492LV00007B/2507

* 9 7 8 8 1 9 5 0 3 5 0 3 8 *